Edges Soft and Sharp

Talia Trentacoste

BookLeaf
Publishing

India | USA | UK

Presentation by *BookLeaf Publishing*

Web: www.bookleafpub.com

E-mail: info@bookleafpub.com

ISBN: 978-93-5744-351-7

First edition 2022

Edges Soft and Sharp

Words from an over-thinker, attempting perfect
rawness
Words from a caricature, lying but so honest
Words from an over-drinker, slurred but crystal
clear
Words from a fantasizer, never really here

Words from a dreamer, claiming chivalry is not
dead
Words from a realist, convinced it's all in her
head
Words from an undertaker, commodifying grief
Words from a romanticizer, wrought with false
belief

Pleas from a lover, clinging onto hope
Tears from a child, dressed in her mother's
clothes
Trickling from a broken glass, desperate to leave
a mark
Poems from a raging storm, edges soft and
sharp.

I Swear I Must Be Changing

How much do I change?
With every ride between
Tower Hill and Temple
How much do I change?
With every airplane meal
I hold in my mouth but do not chew
How much do I change?
With every tear I suck back in
When I alight from the Northern Line
At Leicester Square
How much do I change?
With every trek across
Tower Bridge
Solo or together
How much do I change?
With every £5.40 pint
How much do I change?
With every night
Alone and cold and drowning
In a man-made pool of tears and sweat
How much do I change?
With every moment
Of eye contact I choose to break
Because one of us has to do it
How much do I change?

Nothing Is You

Everything feels like you
Cold wind and lukewarm showers
Three squares in a row beneath my feet
80 kilo footsteps on my shoulders
The rush of air
At the platform edge
The rush of blood
Alone in my bed

Everything tastes like you
Vodka coke white wine cheap beer
Eggs on toast with hot sauce
Lamb curry, melting on my tongue

Everything smells like you
My soap
My sweat
My breath
Mixed with yours
The rain on the floor

Everything sounds like you
Music that I don't even like
Crackling microphone
The voice on the tube

Everything looks like you
Dark hair
Dark suits
Dark sky
The dark
Indent in my mattress

The air I breathe
Sweetened by you
The streets I walk
Bruised by you

But a ghost is not a soul
And a breeze does not console
Not when everything
Looks sounds smells tastes feels
Like you

And certainly not when
Nothing is you.

Wild Winter's Blow

Wild winter's blow
You should wrap your scarf up tighter
Melt summer's frozen nose
Strike your heart to build a fire

The leaves have all been dead here
Since man first climbed a tree
We'll have improved ones in the New Year
(Batteries sold separately)

We've dried up all the nectar
And squeezed all of the lemons
We're burning at the altar
And still fearful of heaven

Every day it seems to be
That hell is climbing higher
And every child's destiny
Turns God into a liar

Astronaut

Sometimes i feel
Like an astronaut…
Do you?
I swear I must be floating
I swear I couldn't possibly be
This close to the sky
If I were on the ground

Sometimes I wish
Someone would join me
In my trip around the sun…
An astronaut with whom
To live in exile

Sometimes I think
Other people must be aliens
There's just no way
We're speaking the same language
Not when I'm saying this,
And you're saying that
(there's just no way)

Sometimes,
But only sometimes,

I just want to touch down

My Body

I am not my body
My body is a vessel
Through which I sing
See
Dance (though terribly)
Shout.

She is curved
Soft hard
Kind angry
Scarred…
Just like the city
Through which she prowls

I carry fifty stars on my back
And with every turn I make
Down the winding, backwards streets
One falls off
And I feel a pound lighter

what i eat in a day (LDN)

Toothpaste and a morning high
Tried to work out, failed.
I've run out of meds so I spiiiiin
And skip to Pret in the station.

Skinny cappuccino for twenty quid a month
Skinny because I am trying to be normal
And pretend that I don't love the fact
That I was pleasantly surprised
When I googled '56 kilos to lbs';
That I wore spandex shorts
In my previously stated attempt
And my fat didn't get all squished;
That I woke up at 2:37am,
Wrote about "the fat
that spills over my ribs,"
Masturbated,
Then fell back to sleep.

A sample of mushroom risotto on my way
Into the market,
It tumbled down, down, down,
Into the bottom of my empty stomach
An acidic rock
I gagged. It tasted wonderful.

Kid goat kofta wrap, Mediterranean
With tzatziki and chili (hot)
For eight pound fifty, courtesy of
Borough Market
And the money of my fellow Westerners

I sat on a step
Apologized to the kind man who
Spat oyster sauce at me
Put in my headphones
And greedily slurped that dead baby goat.

Now that mushroom risotto
Swims with the goat
And the onion
And the pita
And the tzatziki
And the chili (hot)
And the lemon juice and the parsley

One scoop of Bath Dairy
Blackcurrant & Clotted Cream
Ice cream. Three pounds.
A bite of the wooden spoon, too.
Delicious.
I could eat the whole tub.
But I won't, because:
1) I'm broke, and

2) that's not very skinny cappuccino of me

Eleven pound fifty for lunch
Because I've run out of my meds
And failed this morning.
Dead goat and tzatziki
Because my sibling tried to die
And [-----] won't admit he contributed.
Decadent milk from Bath cows
Frozen and sweet
Because the only thing I am good for is sex.
(A landing strip for clotted cream)
Tears on London Bridge
Because I can't stop spinning
And because they taste salty
And because I'm not hungry anymore
But that won't stop me from eating.
Track one of some celebrity's new album
(Couldn't stomach it)

I crawl to Bank
And stumble upon a protest
"Free Palestine!" they shout
"I dreamt that my sister got killed
For being a queer Jew!" I scream
In my head
"Free Palestine!" I shout, craving
the Israeli latkes
I passed at Borough Market

And hating myself
For it

A splinter of wood from
my picket sign,
£1.50 towards
climate justice,
The metallic cream of blood,
Because this time it's
Me who got shot
In my head

Another skinny cappuccino from Pret
On the way home,
Because I am a shit person.
And because I needed a table
On which to write this

Tesco Express Butter
And probably some Jammie Dodgers.
Maybe I'll eat those and
Polish off that pack of Digestives
When I get home

Neapolitan Ice Cream

You can have a cake
And eat it too
I am everlasting
Baked at 500°F

I am tough
Bread crust
I am clever
Warm butter
I am affectionate
Lemon cake
And bold
Chocolate frosting
And honest
Birthday candles

I am Neapolitan ice cream
Have a taste.

Mirror

Say hello to the person in the mirror
An indistinguishable shape
of cream and brown.
Give her a wave, a wink.
Give her a smile, a frown.

Ask her all the things
she would never ask herself
like
Are you okay?
Are you ashamed?
Why don't you ask for help?

Are you still too loud?
Are you still too brave?
Or did you lose yourself
in those addicting waves?

The towering, dark water
crashes over you and pulls you deep.
Did they have to drag you under,
or did you go willingly?

Do you do things because you want to

or just because you can?
Do you seek out food you like
or eat whatever's there?
Do you spend time with people 'cause you want
to
or because you're lonely and they're there?

Do you dance with reckless fire
and does she ever burn your hands?
Do you reach with golden fingers,
touch everything you can?
Or do you lose yourself, like I do, in all the
Things I can't.

Have you ever fed yourself strawberries?
Have you ever held your own hand?
Have you ever woken up early
to meet the sun
and help her kiss the land?

If you could fly,
would you ever land?

You know you shouldn't give too much
but you love to be used up.
So you say "who can spread me thinnest?"
and you do it anyway.

Are you spinning, climbing, falling, floating

like you were yesterday?

Are you praying to no one again?
You know that never helps.
You plead for it to get better
Ask for a sign from a higher realm.
But if you don't believe in anyone up there
Only you can save yourself.

Are you coughing from all the dust
That's gathered on your shelf?

Are you running for fear of stopping
Or for fear of fear itself?

Are you the person I always wanted you to be?
You're shaking your head "no,"
I say, "how disappointing,"
and all you say is
"oh"

Do you feel the gold and orange
Rushing suddenly into you?
Like a foreign bird
Born from brightest blaze,
Holding high its fiery plume.

Then, in a second, do you feel it fly away?
Do you grab its tail? Do you watch it go?

It takes the air, leaving cold behind,
Bringing with it that gilded glow.

I can see it now: the heavy weight
Of your eyelashes on your cheeks.
I'm here on the bathroom floor
An unlucky – no, lucky – interferer
Conversing with and distracting the girl
Who's trapped behind the mirror.

Lost

How is it that you
Make me ignore what I have
And forget what I have not?

How is it that I
Blindly let you take my hand
When I knew you were just as lost?

Explain to me because
I know
You wouldn't take it back.
Even if you made me erase
Those lines
You claim we crossed.

Tell me please
Will you love me
If I keep my hair long?
If I cut my nails short?
If I let my tongue loose or bite it back?
If I hold my eyes open even when it hurts too
bad?
If I blink back tears and tell you that I cried?
If I find myself lost
And tell you that I tried?

Gold Twine

Take a breath
Savor it before
We chase it away
Again

Keep your eyes open
I know it's hard
But if they close
You'll regret it
When the visions fade
And the feelings
Dissipate

I won't let you be satisfied
I won't let you be warm
I'll keep the window open
There's always room to grow

Maybe if you are not satisfied
You will stay longer and
Maybe if you are cold
You will come closer

And the golden rule:
DON'T check the time!

Please please please don't
Just stay right where you are and never ever
leave

Sometimes I think you're made up
Or you're fucking with me
Or this is a big, long dream

Can we just stay here?
Enveloped in
Gold twine.

Ode to Joy

O Say, Can You See
By The Dawn's Early Light…

Fifty stars for the
Fifty different brands of peanut butter
Thirteen stripes for the
Thirteen soda size options

Hospitals the size
Of Aldgate Station
Costcos the size
Of King's Cross
Prisons the size
Of the O2 Arena

Fifty stars for the
Fifty billionaires
And the fifty thousand homeless people.
Thirteen stripes for the
Thirteen thoughts and prayers
And the thirty encouraging Instagram posts
Directed at the people on whose
Shoulders you are standing.

The subway system

A simple collection of pipelines:
Segregated school
To prison,
Bribery
To presidency,
Gay marriage
To Hell,
Abortion
To exile,
Innocence
To gunpoint,
Home
To literally as far away from home as you can
possibly get,
Society-sanctioned depression
To the pavement below the window
Of your eleventh-floor apartment.

Oh, how terrible our trains are!
They rattle
And shake
And they never feel safe
And they can barely carry you
From place to place

Fifty stars for the
Fifty bullets
Embedded in someone more innocent
Than the hero holding the gun.

Thirteen stripes for the
Thirteen bars
Trapping
American Dreamers.

Promise

How could you have promised
To bring me to see the stars
Knowing it would only be
One month
Before they're taken down?

How could you have promised
To hold me up and hold me close
Knowing it's only been
One month
Since I lost balance
And gained control?

How could you have promised
That it was never just false hope
Knowing I would only need
One thread
Of doubt to break this rope?

I'm walking beneath those stars today.
It's colder now, it's Christmas now,
And the ghost of our hands intertwined
Sends a shiver of wind
Through the LED sky

If I blink I swear I can see you
Clearly
But the hand in yours
Is no longer mine
How could you promise?
Why would you promise?

My friends are dating each other
And they're laughing up ahead
And they're gonna have great sex later tonight
And they're bundled up in gold twine
I take one moment
To fall away,
Out of this snow globe…

I take one moment
Just to pray,
To a god I've never known,
That you haven't promised
To bring her here
And you haven't promised
To hold her up
And you haven't promised
It's not false hope
And if you have,
That you break that promise
The way I know you can

And then I take one moment

To swallow the bile
That's risen in my throat
And the hatred
(Not at you, never at you)
Hidden beneath my coat

How could you have promised
To bring me to see the stars
Knowing it would only take
Five words
For you to take me
Right down with them?

God I'm So Fucking Sick of Men!

[see title]

Big Pretty Arms

I tremble and shiver under your weight
I do what I always do,
I hold you at arm's length
Then I pull you into me
A deep embrace

I say "it has never hurt this bad"
As I stab myself in the back
You hold me and wrap your
Big pretty arms
Around me and around the knife
And you say
"Yes it has"

You're the only one I turn to
And you trick me into thinking
I'm in love

Tied Up

I swear to god
I'm locked in place
This must be a trick
This much be a test

There's just no way
This can be real
I am the main character
In a book
Of choose your own adventure

"I call it the empath's double bind…"
Please please please stop talking
It hurts too much
Please please please go on
I feel seen I feel hurt I feel heard

So here I am
On the cusp of my third decade
Double bound
By me, by you, by all of them
Those I fled
Left behind
And those I choose to allow

To scare me
One day I'll probably
Flee from them
Leave them behind
Too

And here I am
On the cusp
Of something that I can taste
And I can feel
But I can't quite see
The lines are blurred
And they only exist
Because you put them there
Just so you could cross them
And apologize
And leave me here
Tied up
And bound in gold twine.

A Sky So Blue

Here I am again
Acting like everything's alright
But it's not
And it hasn't been
Since day one.
Acting like it's not
Way too soon
To be fucking this up.

Sometimes I just have to close my eyes
And think about
Where I can safely step.
Am I in love with you
Or am I in love with
The way I lose my breath?

Sometimes I just have to
Close my eyes
And push down a flare of anger.
How dare you offer to sleep on the floor?
When you know
I don't want that and I've never
Wanted you more.

But it's all water

Under the bridge we crossed
The hand I dropped
The fight you lost
The fat that spills
Over my ribs,
The way you make me feel
Like a kid.

Does the moon tire
Of running away from the sun?
And will my poor soul tire
Of waiting for the one?
Because I know
The sun is sick of seeing
The sky so blue
And my friends
Are tired of hearing
How it's not you.

Promise (cont.)

I didn't do it maliciously

                              You

hurt me
I didn't mean to

                              You

made me ache
…

                              You

confuse me
I confuse me too

                              …

No we're not

                              I heard

differently.
…

                              …

I promise not to overstep

                              Please
                              Please
                              Please
                              Please

don't promise that.

Prosecco

Tree trunk thighs
Washboard backs
Beanstalk legs
Ballpoint pen fingers
Riding crop arms
(And me)

Glass after glass of
Prosecco and champagne

Snarled lips and wide grins
Blank eyes and booming laughs
Furrowed brows and crinkled cheeks
Dirty hands and white teeth

And glass after glass of
Prosecco and sham pain

Thirty-Five Hundred

Autumn winds
Cut like a knife
Icy branches
Choose their victims wisely

Hat and mittens
Static hair and cracked knuckles
Too cold and not shivering enough
Too warm and not hot enough
Ten thousand feet high
And thirty-five hundred miles away

Located and tracked and triangulated
Caught in a web that I spun myself

Wishlist

I miss my bed I miss my blanket I miss my
mirror
I miss my furnace
I miss big pretty arms and
Loss of breath and
Warm strong legs and
Triple vodka coke and
Electricity sparks and
Lukewarm showers and
Too much pasta and
Cheap sandwiches and
Fake pretending and
Easy anger and easy answers and
Daily surprises and nightly presents and future
gifts
All wrapped up with gold twine
Stuffed animals and
Razor blades and
Edges soft and sharp.

www.ingramcontent.com/pod-product-compliance
Lightning Source LLC
La Vergne TN
LVHW010934200726
843509LV00013B/2211